FOCUSING:

BLACK MALE-FEMALE RELATIONSHIPS

D0282322

FOCUSING:

BLACK MALE-FEMALE RELATIONSHIPS

DELORES P. ALDRIDGE

Third World Press . Chicago

Focusing: Black Male Female Relationships

by Delores P. Aldridge, Ph.D.

THIRD WORLD PRESS
CHICAGO, IL.

First edition 1991
First printing 1991
ISBN: 0-88378-140-9
LC#: 91-65326
Cover art and design by Wyatt Hicks

Manufactured in the United States of America
Third World Press
7524 S. Cottage Grove Avenue
Chicago, IL 60619

To all men and women of African descent who take pride in that lineage, and especially to Kwame Essuon, my husband for the last nineteen years.

PREFACE

Focusing: Black Male-Female Relationships serves as a companion volume for an earlier one entitled *Black Male-Female Relationships: A Resource Book of Selected Works,* published by Kendall/Hunt Publishers, 1989. The Sourcebook is a collection of selected published works, while *Focusing* is singularly authored and seeks to examine significant work in the area by "honing in on" or "focusing upon" the critical dimensions shaping Black male-female relationships.

This volume, then, attempts to analyze selected descriptive writings and empirical work found primarily in the social science literature over the past decade and a half – a time span during which many analyses of the lives of Black people, in general, were conducted. The book uses the exploration of scholarly works as a background for constructing a grand theoretical framework that should prove useful for approaching an understanding of Black male-female relationships, while crystallizing fertile areas for future research and policy development. Although it is hoped that the work will provide a framework for research and policy development, the volume should also be of value to individuals who have been engaged in the helping professions, who have been involved in their own relationships, or simply, who are interested in this timely and often provocative subject area. Thus, it is offered as a work for all concerned with human interaction in the modern world.

ACKNOWLEDGEMENTS

Acknowledgements are made to the countless number of students, colleagues and friends who have provided encouragement and criticism of my ideas on male-female relationships over the last decade. Special acknowledgement is made to the students of my first Black male-female seminar at Emory. And, of course, I am indebted to Pearl Holley for typing this and many other manuscripts.

TABLE OF CONTENTS

The relationship between man and man, man and woman, man and children will be clarified and re-defined once the Black man and woman involve themselves in the genuine struggle of the Black world. As long as they remain apart from it, doing their *own* thang, by definition, *our* thang will never be completed.

Haki Madhubuti
From Plan to Planet
Life Studies: The Need For African Minds
and Institutions
1973

INTRODUCTION

The increasing attention dedicated to describing and explaining Black male-female relationships is characterized both by its problem-centered emphasis and a lack of consensus concerning the causes of the problems. Less energy is spent constructing concise frameworks for empirically-based future research and policy development concerning Black male-female relationships.

Problems in Black male-female relationships are most frequently approached in terms of racism and sexism (Sizemore, 1973; Karenga, 1982; Staples, 1979; Wallace, 1979, 1982; and Gary, 1981). Another problem-centered approach utilizes the demographic scarcity of Black men (Jackson, 1978; Braithwaite, 1981; Staples, 1981). Game playing (Staples, 1978; Burgest and Goosby, 1985) as well as inequities in the American economy confronting partners and potential spouses (Staples, 1981) form two additional problem foci that are considered to adversely affect Black male-female relationships. Myths, stereotypes and properties of relationships (Rodgers-Rose, 1980; Gary, 1985) are yet another area of problem definition.

At the institutional level, the interplay of racism, sexism, capitalism and Judeo-Christianity (Aldridge, 1984) on individuals form a more embracing theoretical umbrella under which the previously mentioned problem areas may be seen as explanatory conceptual frameworks, albeit at a lower level of abstraction. Also it is clear that at the interpersonal level the need for examining individual behavior and expectations is crucial. Combined, then, the interpersonal and institutional factors form a broad framework for understanding Black male-female relationships.

This book responds to the challenge of selecting descriptive and empirical writings of social science scholars as a necessary prelude to developing a macrotheory, which can initiate further research, generate carefully designed hypotheses and, finally, evolve research-based policies that will address Black male-female problems. It is important the reader understands the position taken here – that societal problems are the reflection of ideologies and institutionalized practices that may very well define the basic sociopsychological fabric of the society. In fact, a line of thinking and research is developing that suggests our approach to "resolving conflicts" and understanding Black male-female relationships may require unraveling several fundamental institutions upon which America was built.

CHAPTER 1

TOWARD A MACROANALYTICAL THEORY ON BLACK MALE-FEMALE RELATIONSHIPS

The assignment given to a group of Black freshmen enrolled in a college Humanities class was, "Write a two page essay on a topic that is of major interest to you." Listed here are excerpts from four of the essays.

A. "What is really important to me is learning what I need to learn so I can get a good job, make a lot of money and buy nice things. What do I mean by 'nice things'? A Mercedes-Benz, a nice home in the right kind of neighborhood and nice clothes."

* * *

B. "Before I came here [the university], I had heard that there were a lot of fine Black men on the campus. Well, I've been to parties, spent time in the Student Union and made certain that the majority of my classes are Black Studies classes. I've met a lot of Black men and everyone that I've dated don't know how to treat a sister. But I've been talking to this white boy who sits next to me in my ECON class. We've been seeing each other for three months. He treats me like a person, like a woman likes to be treated. My mother always said that 'Black men ain't shit!'"

* * *

C. "I can't stand the pushy women in this class! They're always talking, cutting you off when you're trying to say something. I mean, the white women know their place in a Black Studies class and keep their mouths closed. But the Black women are always jumping in and trying to put the brothers down."

* * *

D. "What's really important to me is that my boyfriend is not aggressive enough in our relationship. I mean, I believe that the man should be the leader and the woman should be the handmaiden to the man. I know that sounds silly, but I've been raised in a Christian home and that's the way that my mother and father act. My father leads and my mother tries to support him in every way that she can.

I did have some problems with my father when I said I wanted to go to college. But my mother really supported me in my decision. You know, I think she would have been a real good student in college."

American society is significantly defined by and developed from four major structural and value systems: capitalism, racism, sexism, and the Judeo-Christian ethic (Anderson and Mealy, 1979; Karenga, 1982; Aldridge, 1984). While there is some question as to whether these can be considered institutions or ideologies, reference shall be made to the four as ideological institutions, given their power within American society. What underlies the term "ideological institutions" is a particular vision of knowledge first advanced by Mannheim:

> .... knowledge is distorted and ideological when it fails to take account of the new realities applying to a situation, and when it attempts to conceal them by thinking of them in categories which are inappropriate (1936, 96).

An ideological institution is a codified and long existing set of social arrangements that forms a basic element of a given society. It follows that such institutions share the distortions inherent in the rationale for their existence. With these definitions in mind, let us proceed to interpret each of the ideological institutions named above through analysis of the students' excerpts.

The first student writes about the importance of learning as it is related to a vocational future, e.g., "learning what I need to learn so I can get a good job." However, the comments that follow indicate the student's thinking is a result of socialization in a capitalist society, to wit: "... make a lot of money." And what is the purpose of making a lot of money? The purpose is to buy "nice things." Nice things are defined as "a Mercedes-Benz, a nice home in the right kind of neighborhood and nice clothes." This thinking is a direct reflection of capitalism, a socio-economic system in which private ownership is the primary means for satisfying human needs.

Perhaps more obvious in the student's thoughts is the strong and continuous pursuit of profit (another essential characteristic of capitalism). Pursuit of profit linked to private ownership has a powerful influence upon the thoughts, emotions and actions that shape human relationships. Yet, it is ironic to find a Black male student in the late 20th century subscribing to the same values that led to the enslavement of his ancestors and made the establishment of this country an act of hypocrisy. Still, does not one become accustomed to finding that one is "an object in the midst of other objects" (Fanon, 1967)? The hypocrisy of the Founding Fathers (in certain cases, the founding of mulatto family strains) stems in large part from their perception of Black people as objects, a perception only available to those who perceive their white identity as object controllers. The moral implications of a people who act from an ethnic identity for which they had little responsibility in molding could well form the substance of a separate work.

The second and third essays bear out the effects of racism and sexism. Racism may be defined as a systematic denial and deformation of a people's history *and* humanity based upon specious concepts and hierarchies of race. (The European-American oppression of African-American peoples carries within it a severe moral contradiction between Christian values and economic beliefs.) Sexism is the ideological institution that involves gender and/or sex as an ascriptive and primary determinant in the establishment, maintenance and justification of relationships and exchanges (Karenga, 1982). The second and third student excerpts betray the communicative relationships powered by racism and sexism. A careful reading of both excerpts also reveals the internalization of racist and sexist beliefs, once again, by the descendants of those who were enslaved and further abused as a result of European-American racist and sexist institutional values.

The fourth excerpt displays the full impact of the Judeo-Christian ethic. Male aggressiveness is enshrined within a narrowly limiting leadership style. Femininity becomes defined as submission to the male. And even though there is a glimmering, by the student, of something not quite right about her mother's role ("I think she would have been a real good student in college"), the student still accepts her view of male-female relationships because she's been raised "in a Christian home." If the Black female embraces the role model emphasized by the Judeo-Christian ethic, she is ready and waiting for a further enactment of inferiority expressed through emotions, thoughts, words, and actions. And since the Black male has never been able, because he has not been allowed, to achieve merit-based leadership roles in proportion to his numbers in the population, notions of the right to leadership becomes corrupted and turned back upon the Black female. Yet it goes beyond that. The Judeo-Christian ethic promotes and reinforces the Black and White female positions as inferior. This degradation is probably nowhere more manifest than in the church itself. According to Grant:

> It is often said that women are the "backbone" of the church. On the surface, this may appear to be a compliment, considering the function of the backbone in the human anatomy. Theresa Hoover prefers to use the word "glue" to describe the function of women in the Black church. In any case, the telling portion of the word "backbone" is "back." It has become apparent to me that most of the ministers who use this term are referring to location rather than function. What they really mean is that women are in the "background" and should be kept there: They are merely support workers (1982, 141).

If these definitions can be accepted, then, we can move toward providing evidence of their manifestation in Black life. Figures 1 and 2 illustrate the conceptual framework. Capitalism, racism, sexism, and the Judeo-Christian ethic appear to directly impact Black male-female relationships. However there are other interactive patterns: capitalism nurtures racism and sexism in Black male-female relations irrespective of Judeo-Christianity, and sexism and the Judeo-Christian ethic are interactive in Black male-female relations – as the latter is based in male dominance over females. While Figure 1 focuses on Black male-female relationships, Figure 2 illustrates aspects of the framework important for looking at non-Black relationships also: capitalism nurtures sexism in non-Black male-female relations where race is not

Figure 1

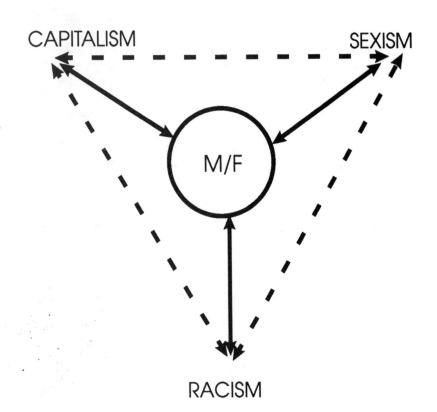

Figure 2

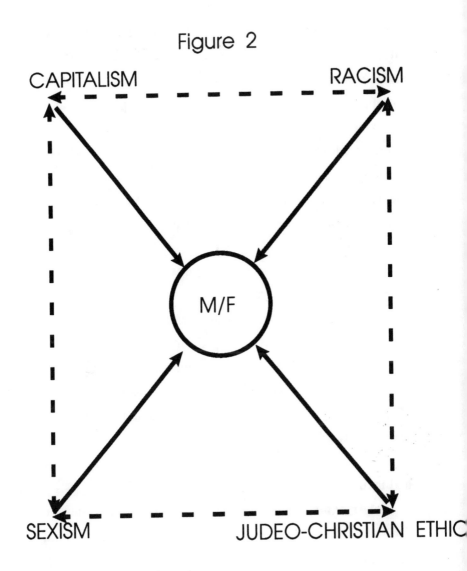

a critical variable. Finally, capitalism, sexism and the Judeo-Christian ethic negatively impact non-Black male-female relations as well. Central to each of these concepts is that of a superior-subordinate status. While capitalism has a dominant theme of owners-workers, racism is rooted in the notion of white superiority and Black inferiority, sexism is defined by male superiority against female inferiority, and one of the major themes of the Judeo-Christian ethic is white male dominance over white females and other race gender groups.

These four ideological institutions furnish the borders within which one may begin to explore Black male-female relationships; capitalism, racism, sexism, and the Judeo-Christian ethic are interlinked and form a power pattern of socialization that results in self and other oppression by Black people upon themselves and each other. The basic irony of Black people buying into this pattern of socialization is that they embrace, unconsciously, the identical pattern of socialization that led to their forced extraction from Africa and their continued oppression in the United States.

An explication of racism, sexism, capitalism, and the Judeo-Christian ethic and their interplay on individual psyches as dominant generating factors for Black male-female problems will place current microanalytical approaches into the larger macroanalytical framework. A closer examination of microanalytical approaches reveals a clustering around two major poles composed of institutional or interpersonal variables, and facilitates an understanding of how these variables anchor and support the macroanalytical approach to Black male-female relationships.

CHAPTER 2

INSTITUTIONAL PERSPECTIVES ON BLACK MALE-FEMALE RELATIONSHIPS

The term "institution" refers to those long standing systematic social arrangements basic to the maintenance of a given society. One speaks of the school, the church and the family as three of America's fundamental institutions. A particular school or church or family is a reflection of the ideal set of social arrangements and expected behaviors that define the respective institutions. Also, institutions must be understood as persisting sets of ideologies or belief systems that organize the ideal social structures and attendant role behaviors, which define both the institutions and the expected behaviors of those involved in institutional arrangements.

This brief introduction to the concept of institution clearly defines institutional racism as a social dynamic affecting the structuring of relationships between Black males and females. It should be understood, however, that the conjunction of institutional capitalism, racism, sexism, and the Judeo-Christian ethic forms what may be termed "institutionalized ideologies." Thus, artificially, we are disaggregating the components for analytical purposes. The social reality remains that of an institutionalized oppressive ideology. What is, perhaps, most important to understand is an institutional view of Black male-female interpersonal relationships that casts the participants as actors performing an institutional script, rather than as active and independent individuals creating their own behaviors.

Racism, Sexism, and Male/Female Relationships

Lawrence Gary, in *Black Men* contends that institutional racism is the most significant perspective from which to study Black males and, implicitly, Black females, as well as the interaction of the two. This perspective, rather than sexism and classism, guides Gary's work. In general, this frame of reference focuses on practices and policies by which Black people, both men and women, are defined as the victims of racism rather than as oppressors. He agrees with Pettigrew, who defines institutional racism as,

> that complex set of institutional arrangements that restrict the life choices of Black Americans in comparison to those of White Americans....Institutional racism avidly supports individual racism .... Racist institutions need not be headed by racists nor designed with racist intentions to limit Black choices. . . . The restrictive consequence is the important fact rather than formal intentions (1973, 274-275).

Gary's view of institutional arrangements rather than independent choice of behaviors enables him to view Black men as neither sexist nor oppressive in their behaviors towards Black women. Racial subordination of Black men, Gary would maintain, negates their advantages as males and restricts the range of much of their expressive behaviors towards Black women. However, Gary concedes that some Black men do oppress some Black women.

Sexism as an institution is studied more thoroughly by others and is viewed by some scholars as a critical variable in explaining the behavior of Black males towards Black females, with the end result of inhibiting and corrupting meaningful relationships. Hare writes:

> ...avowed black feminists have not fomented one unique demand and in general mistake conflicts or difficulties with males in heterosexual relations with feminism. While the white feminist complains that the white male is getting too much, many black feminists see sexism in the black male's

failure to thrive in the market place – the antithesis of feminism. Yet this antithesis will lurk behind and give momentum to the feminist-inspired attacks on black males. Some attack black males for past sexist practices by the white male dominated establishment; for instance, the fact that black female novelists were not published as frequently as black male writers in the past (1989, 167).

The criticism of sexism among Black people has in the past ten years become an issue threatening the strength of the Black community through ideological assaults upon the Black male (Staples, 1979).

Hare contends:

> In the end, what, the black woman wants from the black man is respect and dependability (honesty, love and trust); beyond that she wants him to provide for his family, once more the opposite of the demands of white feminists seeking the right to provide for themselves. From the white man, the black woman wants respect also, but on a less intimate plane; and it is there where her demands for equal job rights and equal pay dovetail with white feminists. Yet, unlike the white feminist, she must deal with racism (including the white feminist's racism), for she is black and woman and, in her dual or pivotal position, is generally aware of the possibility of being used against the race (1989, 167).

Staples (1979) sees the issue of female equity as involving personal relationships as well as political and economic relationships. Thus, he makes the connection with what we would view as more basic American ideological institutions, i.e., sexism, racism and capitalism.

Similarly, Karenga (1982) criticizes the social structure of the United States as a contributing factor to present Black male-female problems, naming the negative influences in society as capitalism, racism and sexism. Yet, his analysis is heightened by his recognition of the manifestation of capitalism, racism, and sexism in four utilitarian and tentative associations, or "connections" (cash, flesh, force and dependency) that defy the formation of long-term and stable relationships by placing tension on Black morality (Karenga, 1982, 219-222). The cash, flesh, force and dependency connections may be severed by a self-conscious struggle by Black men and women to seek moral standards positive to their interests. Without explicitly discussing historical occurrence, Karenga urges Black men and women to remember the quality relationships of the ancestors and to pattern their actions in accordance with the primary concerns and objectives of male-female relationships. Karenga's major assumption is that Black men and women have, to a large extent, accepted the value system of European-American society – a value system that was not designed for the healthy promotion and development of people of African descent.

If a case can be made for institutional racism and sexism as primary motivators in the difficulties that define *some* Black male-female relationships (we have no definitive data as to frequency), it would appear that we also need to question whether there is a need to restructure the process of

Black male and female socialization. Such a re-education would involve Black females *and* Black males in a shared learning experience, rather than Black females only speaking to each other about Black males. The latter stance involves Black women in a tripartite battle against sexism, racism and capitalism.

Racism and capitalism are forces that have subjected Black women to political and economic subordination. Several Black authors have used this explanatory approach in recent years (e.g., Anderson and Mealy, 1979). They contend that the Black male-female conflict is a function of America's capitalistic tradition and historic subjugation of Black people. Staples (1979) is among those who view feminism as a divisive force in an oppressed community (such as Black America). There are other points of view. Lorde (1979) supports feminism, arguing that since Black women bear the brunt of sexism, it is in their interest to abolish it. She contends that Black women must decide if sexism in the Black community is pathological. According to Lorde, the "creative relationships of which Staples speaks are to the benefit of Black males, considering the sex ratio of males and females." Salaam (1979) joins the discussion insisting the struggle against sexism is not a threat to Black masculinity because the forces that attack Black women individually, institutionally and ideologically also assault Black men.

Still, others, both men and women, have spoken out against feminism (Larue, 1970; Duberman, 1975). The arguments they advance are (1) Black people as a race need to be liberated from racism, (2) feminism creates negative competition between the Black male and the Black female for economic security, (3) White women are the recipients of the benefits of this struggle from Black women; and, (4) feminism facilitates increased tension in the already strained interpersonal atmosphere where Black men and Black women interact.

One might argue, in light of the views presented above, that women's liberation – as it is presently defined and implemented – has a negative impact on the Black liberation movement and on Black male and female relationships. The essence of this writer's disagreement with women's liberation is the basically conservative mode of its beliefs and functions. Women's liberation operates within the capitalist tradition and accepts the end goals of sexist white males; simply stated, women's liberation strives to place women on an equal par with men without considering whether the male position – the white male position – is basically a humanizing position. Black women are victims of capitalism and sexism. How, then, will the relations between Black males and females be bettered through female adherence to a male-defined path? Black liberation must involve males and females openly and courageously seeking mutual liberation; Black liberation cannot have the luxury of a liberation movement operating inside the capitalistic tradition and seeking goals defined by perpetuators of the sexist tradition. Therefore, it will be seen that Black liberation, especially within Black male-female relations, has a far more complex task than women's liberation. Black liberation seeks the establishment of a lovingly free movement within and between Black males and Black females, which re-creates both parties, establishes a tradition that is non-exploitative and non-sexist and draws from the cultural experiences of free Black people (Aldridge, 1984).

Fundamental to the institutional perspective are descriptions and explanations of the Black gender ratio imbalance as well as racial discrimination. Both are manifest most glaringly in income inequality and unemployment. At the interpersonal level, the different socialization of males and females, parental stress in meeting needs – such as adequate food, clothes and shelter – and the male superiority or male double standards are most often cited. It is important to note that these explanations are differentially applied in discussing various income and age groups.

TABLE 1

Sex Ratio of the Nonmarried Black Population 18 Years and Over: 1972, 1977, 1982, 1987

Sex Ratio for Total Population

	1972	1977	1982	1987
Male	2,490,000	3,221,000	4,144,000	4,645,000
Female	3,893,000	4,827,000	6,060,000	6,699,000
Sex Ratio	64	67	68	69

Sex Ratio by Age

Age

Year	18-19	20-24	25-29	30-34	35-39	40-44	45-54	55-64	65+
1972	101	96	63	64	48	71	46	47	38
1977	93	90	79	59	44	54	64	55	43
1982	95	93	81	65	73	48	55	53	34
1987	93	93	86	78	63	65	47	60	35

Source: U.S. Bureau of the Census, Marital Status and Living Arrangements, Series P-20, Nos. 242, 323, 349, 380, 389, 399, and 418.

The Influence of Demographics on Relationships

The demographic thesis advanced by Jackson (1971) speaks to the outcomes of social institutions rather than demography as an institution. According to Jackson, there has been a fairly consistent decline in the number of Black males available to Black females since 1850. As Table 1 reflects, the gender imbalance has persisted into the seventies and eighties. Since 1972, the number of adult Black male singles available to adult Black female singles (64 males per 100 females) only has continued to increase. More significantly, the sex ratio declines as one moves from the younger to the older ages. For example, with the exception of the 40-44 age group, there was a decline in the sex ratio for the age groups ranging from 18 to 65+ in 1972.

As would be anticipated, the sex ratio vacillated for some of the groups. In general, however, the male shortage is a reality for all age groups. It is an outstanding reality for age groups 20 years and older. Despite the defects that may exist in the statistical data sources, the male-female ratio indicates that more Black females than Black males are available for meaningful relationships.

The implications of this imbalance in the sex ratio for Black male-female relationships are obvious: Black women are at a disadvantage in the mating game. Consequently, the Black male shortage generates intense competition among Black females. Staples (1978) estimated that for specified age groups in particular geographical regions, the Black male-female ratio was one to five. Given this ratio, females are negotiating on the male's terms or stated otherwise, females are buyers in a seller's market.

According to Staples (1981), the effects of the gender imbalance is a particularly difficult issue for college-educated Black women. Aside from the fact that Black women in general prefer to date and marry individuals of similar age and educational status, they also set other often unrealistic standards for their potential mates. Staples (1981) observed that if a Black woman desired a mate who is over six feet tall, a non-smoker with similar or higher educational attainment and with no criminal record, she will have eliminated thousands of single Black men. Many of the men who would satisfy these criteria would already be married or seriously committed to someone else. Such expectations on the part of college-educated Black women only serve to intensify the competition for available Black men. While some Black women have reacted to the Black male shortage by parenting outside of marriage (Jackson, 1971), some are sharing

TABLE 2

**Income for Individuals 14 Years Old and Over by Sex and Race:
1970-1985**

Year	Male Black[1]	White	Female Black[1]	White	Ratio of Black Male to White	Ratio of Black Female to White
1970	4,220	7,011	2,084	2,265	0.60	0.92
1971	4,343	7,237	2,192	2,448	0.60	0.90
1972	4,811	7,814	2,502	2,616	0.62	0.96
1973	5,318	8,453	2,626	2,823	0.63	0.93
1974	5,689	8,854	2,858	3,117	0.64	0.92
1975	5,861	9,300	3,158	3,420	0.63	0.92
1976	6,216	9,937	3,420	3,606	0.63	0.95
1977	6,483	10,603	3,538	4,001	0.61	0.88
1978	7,297	11,453	3,801	4,117	0.64	0.92
1979	7,974	12,305	4,091	4,393	0.65	0.93
1980	8,354	13,228	4,732	4,947	0.63	0.96
1981	9,068	14,296	5,073	5,519	0.63	0.92
1982	9,493	14,748	5,341	5, 967	0.64	0.90
1983	9,758	15,401	5,709	6,424	0.63	0.89
1984	10,394	16,467	6,353	6,949	0.63	0.91
1985	11,350	17,111	6,473	7,357	0.66	0.88

[1]Black and other non-white races

Source: U.S. Bureau of the Census, Current Population Reports, Series p. 60, Nos. 146, 151, and 156.

partners (Chapman, 1986; Scott, 1976) and others are lacking any meaningful relationships (Karenga, 1982).

Inequities in the American Economy

Some social scientists maintain that at the core of the problems in Black dating and marital relationships is the perennial difficulty obtaining jobs and adequate incomes necessary for satisfying relationships. For many years, the median income of Black males and Black females 14 years old and over has lagged behind that of their white counterparts (Table 2).

In the last decade and a half, the median income of Black males never reached two-thirds of the median income of white males. Perhaps, even more striking is the fact that the income gap has repeatedly shown signs of widening. Although Black females appear to compare more favorably with white females than Black males with white males, in reality, they fare worse than either one of the other three groups. More important, when differences in employment status (Table 3) and educational attainment (Table 4) are taken into account, the income gap still persists.

TABLE 3

Income for Year-round, Full-Time Workers 14 Years Old and Over by Sex and Race:

1970-1985

Year	Male		Female		Ratio of Black Male to White	Ratio of Black Female to White
	Black [1]	White	Black [1]	White		
1970	6,638	9,447	4,664	5,536	0.70	0.84
1971	7,006	9,905	5,192	5,767	0.71	0.90
1972	7,576	10,918	5,341	6,172	0.69	0.87
1973	8,298	11,800	5,724	6,958	0.70	0.87
1974	9,320	12,399	6,805	7,235	0.75	0.94
1975	10,151	13,233	7,598	7,737	0.77	0.98
1976	10,478	14,272	7,884	8,376	0.73	0.94
1978	12,943	16,360	9,101	9,732	0.79	0.94
1979	13,558	17,984	9,875	10,623	0.75	0.93
1980	14,757	19,720	10,960	11,703	0.75	0.94
1981	15,771	21,178	11,604	12,665	0.74	0.92
1982	16,710	22,232	12,577	13,847	0.75	0.91
1983	17,451	23,114	13,318	14,677	0.75	0.91
1984	18,294	24,826	14,494	15,575	0.74	0.93
1985	19,039	25,693	14,990	16,482	0.74	0.91

[1] Black and other non-white races

Source: U.S. Bureau of the Census, Current Population Reports, Series P-60, 1970-1985.

TABLE 4

Education and Income —Year Round, Full-Time Workers 18 Years Old and Over by Sex and Race: 1975-1985

Male

	Black			White		
Years	Elementary 8 Years	High School 4 Years	College 4 or More	Elementary 8 Years	High School 4 Years	College 4 or More
1975	9,552	10,171	13,418	10,592	12,921	18,321
1976	9,340	10,278	15,211	11,312	13,587	19,171
1977	8,208	10,821	15,535	12,266	14,786	20,510
1978	9,271	12,645	17,702	13,082	15,644	21,900
1979	11,912	13,155	19,598	14,228	17,051	23,803
1980	11,774	15,658	20,335	15,064	19,857	26,139
1981	12,112	16,014	21,424	16,558	20,968	28,648
1982	13,462	16,469	21,520	16,773	21,856	30,521
1983	12,129	16,820	26,606	16,892	22,351	32,137
1984	14,109	16,724	28,244	17,113	24,000	34,403
1985	14,192	18,452	27,858	19,069	24,822	36,110

Female

	Black			White		
Years	Elementary 8 Years	High School 4 Years	College 4 or More	Elementary 8 Years	High School 4 Years	College 4 or More
1975	4,733	7,454	10,158	5,856	7,283	11,067
1976	5,557	7,778	12,057	6,461	7,931	11,685
1977	5,748	8,185	12,614	6,617	8,493	12,251
1978	6,974	8,936	12,113	7,542	9,182	12,984
1979	7,046	9,297	15,088	7,841	9,996	14,319
1980	–	11,008	16,082	9,101	11,636	16,441
1981	8,150	11,527	16,069	10,181	12,455	18,085
1982	8,199	12,105	17,240	10,572	13,458	19,586
1983	9,128	12,413	18,848	10,725	13,989	20,382
1984	10,804	13,619	21,222	10,849	14,733	22,089
1985	11,987	13,806	20,832	11,347	15,715	23,517

-Not available , number in work force less than 75,000.
Source: U.S. Bureau of the Census, Current Population Reports, Series P-60, 1975-1983.

Admittedly, the income gap closes to approximately three-quarters of the white male rate for Black males with various educational statuses, and to nearly nine-tenths for Black females. It is depressing to observe that white males with eight years of elementary school education are likely to earn more than Black males with four years of high school education.

Aside from the income gap, a considerably larger number of Blacks than whites are unemployed. In spite of the recent announcements about declines in the unemployment rates, the situation is far worse for Blacks than for any other group, especially when considering the fact that the pool of discouraged workers does not get entered into the computations. While more Blacks are unemployed than whites, equally significant is that those employed tend to be in less prestigious, insecure jobs. This fact takes on greater significance if considered in the context that one's employment influences to a large extent the way others view him/her and in turn, the way he/she sees himself/herself. In this light, job satisfaction becomes a major factor influencing marital satisfaction and the overall satisfaction with life. A steady job potentially serves as a personal stabilizing force and hence, contentment with one's marital relationships. Franklin (1986) concludes:

> Our society today undoubtedly remains structured in such a manner that the vast majority of Black men encounter

insurmountable barriers to the attainment of a "masculine" status as defined by most Americans (Black and White Americans). Black men still largely are locked within the Black culture (which has relatively limited resources), unable to compete successfully for society rewards – the attainment of which defines American males as "men." Unquestionably, Black men's powerlessness in society's basic institutions such as the government and the economy contributes greatly to the pathological states of many Black men. The high morality and suicide rates of young Black men, the high incarceration rates of Black men, and the high unemployment rate of Black men are all functions of societal barriers to Black male upward mobility. These barriers render millions of Black males socially impotent and/or socially dysfunctional (110).

Liebow, in his book, *Tally's Corner: A Study of Negro Street Corner Men* provides this insight:

The way in which the man makes a living and the kind of living he makes have important consequences for how the man sees himself and is seen by others; and these, in turn importantly shape his relationship with family members, lovers, friends, and neighbors. Making a living takes on an overriding importance at marriage. Although he wants to get married he hedges his commitment from the very beginning because he is afraid not of marriage itself, but of his own ability to carry out his responsibilities as a husband and father. His own father failed and had to "cut out" and the men he knows who have been or are married have also failed or are in the process of doing so. He has no evidence that he will not. The black menial worker remains a menial worker so that after one or two or three years of marriage and as many children, the man who could not support his family from the very beginning is even less able to support it as time goes on. The longer he works, the longer he is unable to live on what he makes. He has little vested interest in such a job and learns to treat it with the same contempt held for it by the employer and society at large. From his point of view, the job is expendable; from the employer's pont of view, he is. Sometimes, he sits down and cries at the humiliation of it all. Sometimes he strikes out at her or the children with his fists, perhaps to lay hollow the claim to being man of the house in the one way left open to him, or perhaps simply to inflict pain on this woman who bears witness to his failure as a husband and father and therefore as a man. Increasingly, he turns to the street corner where a shadow system of values constructed out of public fictions serves to accomodate just such men as he, permitting them to be men once again provided they do not look too closely at one another's credentials (1967: 210 - 213).

Sizemore (1973) does not mince words as she posits that the highest status in American society is afforded to white, wealthy males. Women who are both Black and poor are given a very low position – one that is strengthened by such stereotypes as the myth of "Black Matriarchy." The plight of Black women is worsened by poverty, which affected nearly one half of all nonwhite families in the decade of the sixties and was at an even higher level in families with the father absent. These poverty circumstances are often complicated when Black males are not aware of the nature of the problems accompanying them, such as limited capacity to demonstrate warmth, restricted verbal communication, and restrained efforts at expressing concern or understanding of a partner's emotional needs. Thus, Black male-female relationships can become combat zones, as opposed to a desired mutually loving and supportive web. Moreover, this inability to be loving when in combat over financial resources does not

obtain simply for the very poor, but cuts across socio-economic lines. For even the "better off" Blacks are not on parity with non-Blacks, although they judge themselves in the context of the larger society (as so well portrayed in various forms of media and elsewhere). Thus, a society that fosters the assessment of one's individual worth, but simultaneously denies equal access to financial rewards for all its citizens, is a nation in need of reassessment.

When the socio-economic reality is placed in this context, certain issues of morality that emerge from the persisting inability of this nation to confront the affects of an institutionalized oppressive ideology become difficult to evade. Specifically, if morality is based upon the individual taking responsibility for his or her choice of actions and the outcomes of those actions, what can we say about an entire society constructed upon a set of identities – Black and White – that, at the physical level, represent identities or "beingness" for which no one is responsible? Or, simply stated, who has asked to be born with a particular color of skin?

Ontology is that branch of philosophy that speaks issues of being. A person's being contains, among of things, his/her identity as an individual and his/her identity a racial being. What, then, does Frantz Fanon mean, in *B Skin, White Masks*, when he says that "every ontology is r unattainable in a colonized and civilized society" (1967

109)? One possible interpretation is that primacy given to one's ethnic being contradicts the achievement or attainability of an individuality. Or, expressed in another manner, one is always an "adjectivized" being (e.g., a *Black* individual, a *White* individual). For if the individual is unique, do we not contradict this uniqueness and even the possibility for healthy psychosocial development of the individual if he or she perceives self and is perceived by others in terms of the controlling adjectives Black and White, particularly where one color is viewed as superior to the other? The implications for immorality – a sense of non-responsibility stemming from a loss of one's sensing of one's self worth – are staggering. But this forms the topic for another work and remains a tantalizing afternote in the discussion of Black male-female relationships.

CHAPTER 3

INTERPERSONAL PERSPECTIVES ON BLACK MALE-FEMALE RELATIONSHIPS

A baby is born knowing nothing, but full of potential. The process by which an individual becomes a creature of society, a socialized human being reflecting culturally defined roles and norms, is complex and as yet imperfectly understood. It is evident, however, that most individuals eventually reflect societal definitions more or less well ... (Chafetz, 1974: 69).

The classical explanation for how an individual's identity emerges and develops is that provided by symbolic interactionists, such as Charles H. Cooley (1909) and George Herbert Mead (1934). Through interaction with "significant others," primarily parents, and, later, peer groups, children develop an idea of self composed of "three principal parts: the imagination of our appearance to the other person, the imagination of this judgment of that appearance, and some sort of self-feeling – such as pride or mortification" (Cooley: 1909, 152). Cooley referred to this as the "looking glass self."

In taking this approach to another level, Mead emphasized the key role of language in the interaction process. He contends that children first develop a sense of "I," namely, a basic awareness of self as actor and organism. Subsequently, the "me" develops, which comprises an understanding and internalization of how others perceive the child. The "me" is the social component of the personality; it embodies the internalization of roles, norms and values presented by society. It is learned by the child through role-playing – taking the role of the other in negotiating human interactions. This can only occur through the manipulation of symbols, that is, language. Through this process, the child learns the organized attitudes and expectations of the larger social groupings, referred to by Mead as "the generalized other." Stated in its most basic form, children learn who they are and internalize what they are expected to be by trying to put themselves in the place of others and experience themselves as others perceive them.

If we learn who and what we are by carefully observing how other people react to us, then, according to Pettigrew, this process is highly structured for Blacks by the roles they are expected to play. When a Black man or woman attempts to gain an image of himself or herself on the basis of his typical contacts with white America, he or she receives primarily negative responses. Banks and Grambs (1972) put it this way:

> for the Black...in white American society, the generalized other whose attitudes he assumes and the looking glass into which he gazes both reflect the same judgment; he is inferior because he is Black. His self-image, developed in the lowest stratum of a color caste system, is shaped, defined, and evaluated by a generalized other which is racist or warped by racists (56).

Two other related concepts are relevant to a discussion of the socialization process. W. I. Thomas (1923) set forth the notion of the "definition of the situation," which recognizes the fact that if human beings define a situation as real, then regardless of objective reality, the fact of defining it has real social consequences. In a society which sends messages that are racist, sexist, capitalist, and have Judeo-Christian ethic roots, the transmission of these messages to Black people can lead to a socializing of their young with noncomplementary values. If for instance, a young Black male is told that "Black boys are useless," regardless of the truth of this assertion, it will have a real impact on that child's behavior and expectations of himself. Robert K. Merton (1957) noted essentially the same phenomenon when he developed the idea of the "self-fulfilling (or destructing) prophecy." Merton's concept applies to those cases where the act of predicting something facilitates the actual occurrence of the phenomenon in question. Accordingly, for example, the female student referred to in the opening chapter, who is told she cannot depend on Black men but must depend upon herself (because Black men are not dependable and Black women must be prepared to make it alone), will probably not acquire a very high regard for Black men or expect very much from them. When later she lacks the ability to appreciate them or highly regard them as dependable individuals and "puts them down" with depreciating behavior towards them, a self-fulfilling prophecy will have been realized. Similarly, if a Black male has been told Black women are "cold, calculating, and evil," and he acts accordingly to illicit that response, the circle is completed where the self-fulfulling prophecy is concerned. We see, once again, an example of the ways in which the oppressed take on "ownership" of the processes by which their oppression continues, the ultimate effectiveness of neo-colonialism (and for many the United States has been a neo-colonialist society in which the oppressed have come to sustain their own oppression).

It is important to add that it is not only Blacks who have fallen into this stifling trap. Many Whites share in the process and suffer the same denial of individuality. A colleague tells a story about a White female student who confessed that she was attracted to a Black male in the class. She could not, she stated, realize her attraction in a dating situation because her parents would object to her dating a Black man.

Thus, she had to deny the reality of her attraction for a male because of the master definition learned from childhood, that this particular male was Black and therefore non-particular and *basically* a Black object. Whether or not the perceived Blackness was the basis for attraction rather than the perception of the other's individuality remains unanswered. Likewise, it remains questionable that we can ever pierce the veil of color to recognize the individual in ourselves or the same or opposite racial Other?

Despite these unanswered questions, it is certain that the success of an institutionalized oppressive ideology is realized when the oppressed assume the task of sustaining their own oppression. Given this fact, the differential patterns of socialization by which sex turns into gender or, otherwise stated, how Black males and Black females are created, must be examined.

Differential Socialization of Males and Females

The difference in childrearing has important implications for adult male-femae relationships. Knowledge of the socialization of males and females provides insight into how each conceptualizes what behavior is appropriate in relating to each other. Differential socialization of Black males and Black females in the early years has the effect of setting them up for conflictual relationships in their adult years (Franklin,

1984). The family serves as the first and most important social agent for the individual. It provides the initial sexual standards and sex roles as the parents serve as role models. Franklin observes that parents and other agents of socialization consciously or unconsciously transmit to Black children noncomplementary gender role definitions, which serve to separate rather than draw Black males and females to one another. Black families promote conflicting definitions of femininity that lead Black women to reject the traditional role of passivity, emotional and economic dependence, while at the same time accepting the feminine role of expressiveness, warmth and nurturance.

Algea Harrison (1974) sets forth the same notion, although somewhat differently. She concludes that not only does the female receive messages from her parents, but she is pressured by the political-economic system and survival needs of the Black community to develop those traits that are contrary to the ideas of womanhood as prescribed by the sex role standard (i.e., independence, self-assertion, persistence). This dual orientation, then, provides a dilemma for Black females that does not facilitate the development of stable relationships.

The relationship between Black men and women does not take place in a vacuum. They act out their behavior in a society that has clearly defined role behavior. According to European-American social definitions, men are supposed to be aggressive and women should be passive. With such a definition of role behavior, based on inequality rather than equality, the relationship between men and women cannot help but be tenuous.

Jourard (1971) explores some critical components of the male role, explaining the socially-defined male role requires men to appear tough, objective, striving, achieving, unsentimental, and emotionally unexpressive. If behind this social persona a man demonstrates any behaviors counter to this description, he will be preceived as lacking strong masculinity traits. The contradiction between the ways Black men are expected to present themselves in small and large group situations and their true emotional feelings is the key to understanding the nature of being a Black male in America. The learned tendency of males to mask their genuine feelings makes it difficult for them to achieve significant insight into and empathy with Black women – a point which Sizemore (1973) makes in discussing sexism and Black males.

To the extent that women require expressions of intimate and personal emotions in a contractual relationship as social or sexual partners, the limited expressive or non-expressive male may find himself in a difficult situation, as observed by Braithwaite (1981). If he is to execute effectively his role as a Black man by involvement with women who demonstrate their attraction to him, he must be fairly adept at something for which he has received contradictory signals (to express emotions of gentleness, tenderness and verbal affection toward women while at the same time personifying an aggressive, strong, unexpressive and cool image.)

According to Braithwaite (1981), the high degree of verbal facility among Black males makes it easier for them to create an initial impression of genuine feelings and to enter into relationships with women. As the relationship continues and the woman becomes more familiar with the male's mannerisms and behavior, it becomes increasingly difficult for the Black male to camouflage his absence of genuine feelings for his partner. In these cases, the male must constantly "pretend," expressing sentiments he really does not feel. Perhaps this is a partial explanation for seemingly bizarre and unanticipated physical attacks upon one's partner followed by loving apologies. The attacks might be explained another way. They could reflect a response to insecurity and fear of losing his "property." Either explanation may result in a terminated relationship, whereby the major issue takes on more clarity. The issue, it appears, is not entering relationships with women, but, rather, sustaining relationships with women once they have been initiated.

Tucker (1978) indicates that success with women is important to many men because they are engaged in covert competition with other men. The belief is that success will enable them to avoid ridicule and to be perceived as "hip."

Given this male/male process, women become targets and the communication structure by which they become targets becomes an end in itself rather than a means to an end. A by-product of this process is self-rejection of those emotions that when displayed may leave one vulnerable.

The rising tide of teen-age pregnancy among all youth may be, in large part, attributable to the objectification of women as sexual objects. Given the high rates of teen-age pregnancy among Black youth, it could be argued that this is simply another symptom of what happens when the individual is narrowly defined in terms of a racial object. The folklore advanced by Whites concerning Black sexuality betrays not only whites' insecurity but is echoed in the lyrics of so many popular "soul" records. A close reading of these lyrics reveals an intense preoccupation with making love as synonymous to being in love. But these lyrics are not being sung by White people. And in this case, White singers are not receiving industry awards for these record sales. It is Black singers who are singing for the pleasure and further socialization of Black people. Here, once again, we see evidence of the oppressed taking on the behaviors that sustain their own oppression.

This pattern of initial contact and verbal gaming takes on special meaning in the context of capitalism and sexism. The woman becomes an object; one gains in profit as one "scores" on an increasing number of women. Likewise, of

57

course, the expression and possession of emotions that might reveal one's self, as well as treat women as feeling individuals, is contradictory, and, thus cannot be pursued if the values associated with capitalism and sexism have been internalized. Understanding these dynamics raises the question, whether the "new morality" is or is not a logical outgrowth of capitalism and sexism, e.g., the body becomes the object of buying and selling – the inner person is reduced to a dancing (either in public or in the bedroom) object available for the man's pleasure with both actors in the dyad being losers in the final analysis.

Tucker's observation makes clear that self-disclosure is a major factor influencing the quality of interaction between Black men and Black women. A necessary prerequisite to self-disclosure and open communication is an absence of negative game playing, which can sour the development and maintenance of healthy relationships. Yet, what limits and dimensions of the self are to be disclosed and communicated? If the American pattern of socialization, due to the capitalistic underpinnings, is anti-self and pro-object, what will we find when we seek to disclose ourselves and communicate that uniqueness to the Other? Does conscious limitation of intimate social relations preclude the priority of the self's value to one's self and to others? Does "being true to one's own race" conceal yet another vestige of an institutionalized oppressive ideology, or does the statement reflect a pride necessary for survival? Or is it simply the case that our society is so deeply founded upon an institutionalized oppressive ideology that there is no room to raise these types of questions? The struggle with the institutionalized oppressive ideology is an ever-present one, as Black individuals strive to feel good about themselves and, subsequently, other Black people. Thus, positive interpersonal relationships demand much effort, study and, without question, a clear understanding of the forces operating against healthy relationships.

Game Playing, Images, and Male-Female Relationships

Malveaux's essay, "Polar Entities Apart," (1971: 48, 49) provides extraordinary insight into interpersonal relations of Black men and women. She found that some college women think they are exploited by Black men and that the exploitation results from childhood socialization into game playing. However, according to Malveaux playing games with each other does not only apply to male-female relationships but "is the way that Black people relate to each other in all walks of life." Malveaux (1971:48) suggests game playing is not a recent phenomenon, contending that "circumstances forced Blacks to fake closeness which intensify unsurfaced animosity; now our feelings have surfaced and we are at each others throats."

59

In an effort to increase the level of consciousness, awareness for positive communication, and interactions in relationships, Burgest and Goosby (1985) analyzed some of the game-playing strategies used in Black male-female relationships. They divided games into two areas, love and power. The games of love demonstrate the myths, stereotypes, and negative assumptions regarding love in the United States and their impact on Black male-female relationships. Their analyses of games of power dramatize the erroneous assumptions Black males and females make about each other. The authors conclude that the combination of negative myths, stereotypes and assumptions, coupled with inherent payoffs, is responsible for destructive social games affecting courtship, marriage, and relationships between Black males and females. The exposure of the games of power and love played between Black males and females on a personal and social basis is designed to dissipate such destructive interactions and facilitate more authentic interpersonal relations.

While the purpose of *Focusing* is to clarify the complexity of relationships for all Black males and females from the onset of dating to the golden years, college-educated Black singles add further complications. Few studies have been conducted in this area, perhaps because Staples (1981) has discussed the "world" of this group in some considerable detail. From Staples' (1981:64-65) perspective, technological, sexual and other revolutions taking place in American society are the major sources of the difficulties in Black male-female relationships. For the college-educated, these changes include the values of individualism and materialism, which translate into a self-centered philosophy and an obsession with material acquisitions. Staples argues that these values, coupled with others, perpetuate a mythology that recognizes singlehood as the best way of life, even though family is still officially promoted as the ideal state for American adults. While both the electronic and print media communicate images reflecting the wonderful world for singles, the larger society also transmits values that encourage people to marry. If the achievement of familyhood as the ideal has merit, the college-educated Black singles find themselves in a dilemma.

Responses to this dilemma are reflected in the complaints voiced by Black males and females about each other. While many Black men and women are involved in mutually rewarding relationships, others admit that they are suspicious of each other's motives and actions. The complaints and suspicions are many and include lack of love, lack of commitment, as well as the frequently voiced perception of college-educated Black women as overly independent and assertive, and Black men as unable to fill a partner's emotional and intellectual needs. (Attendant to this thinking is the belief that Black women professionals intimidate Black men by the success they have achieved.) Some of these perceptions were supported by a study conducted by Cazenave (1983). In a survey of 155 middle-class men ranging in age from 22-83 years, a majority reported feelings of strained relationships and antagonism resulting from perceptions that Black women had more opportunity than Black men. Similar findings were reported by Watson, Smith and Williams (1984). These three researchers administered a questionnaire containing ten presuppositions about Black female economic superiority to 55 male and 86 female undergraduates and compared the respondents beliefs with corroborative data from the U.S. Department of Labor and Census Bureau. The sample included 84 Black and 57 white respondents. Results show that all respondents, especially Black respondents, were carriers of myths about the differential economic status of Black females and males. Although respondents believed that Black females earn more than Black males, the labor and census data showed that earnings of Black males historically have been and continue to be higher than those of Black females. Tables 1, 2, 3, and 4 show the income advantage of males relative to females, which transcends age and education.

Myths, Stereotypes and Properties of Relationships

In 1977, Wilkinson addressed stigmatization or systematic branding of Black males in a highly acclaimed work, *The Black Male in America* (Wilkinson and Taylor). She stated that stigmas and stereotypes about the Black male are diffused in American racial mythology by means of cultural indoctrination or socialization. She contends that stigmatizing behaviors directed toward Blacks are viewed as patterned and designed processes which have had a measurable impact on the Black male psyche (119).

Other scholars, such as Rodgers-Rose (1980), have examined stigmatization and attempted to explain the linkage to Black male-female relationships. Rodgers-Rose (1980) devotes a chapter to the dialectics of Black male-female relationships in which she focuses upon some myths about Black men and women and properties of male-female relationships. She indicated that most sociologists have studied the outward status characteristics of income, education, occupation, and sexual compatibility. Also, they have studied the first three properties of intimate relationships (conversation, monetary exchange, and sexual intercourse), but they have paid little attention to the fourth property (qualities wanted in a relationship). In the study which Rodgers-Rose conducted, she found that Black males and females were concerned with inner qualities of the individual rather than outward qualities. Even the quality of sexual compatibility does not rank as high as the qualities of honesty, understanding, independence, and proper manners.

Empirically, Gary, like Rodgers-Rose, explores the quality of male-female relationships from the perspectives of Black men and women. His specific research questions were (1) to what extent do Black adults perceive conflict in male-female relationships, and, (2) what factors are associated with such perceptions? The survey consisted of a probability sample of 451 Black adults residing in Richmond, Virginia, 61% females and 39% males. The dependent variable was perception of conflicts in male-female relationships and the independent variables were sex, age, marital status, employment status, income, education (socio-demographic variables), family structure, community participation, religiosity (socio-cultural variables), depressive symptoms and stressful life events (mental health outcome variables).

The major conflicts identified in the sample were lack of communication, lack of feelings, and lack of respect. Among the demographic variables, only education was significantly related to perceived male-female conflict. The college-educated respondents were more likely to perceive conflicts between males and females than were their less educated counterparts. In sum, the findings suggest that level of education, level of depressive symptoms and the number of stressful life events encountered by an individual are key factors in understanding the perception of conflicts in Black male-female relationships.

CHAPTER 4

STRATEGIES FOR BUILDING HEALTHY RELATIONSHIPS

The survival of the Black family rests upon the promotion and development of healthy Black male-female relationships. Karenga (1982) noted that not all Black male-female relationships are in trouble, but a significant number are problematic and, thus, require attention.

> Meaningful relationships can be begun and sustained when they are anchored in common proactive values, common interests and aspirations, quality commitment, support structures, continuous renewal, and common struggle for liberation and a higher level of human life. Without open discussion, egalitarian exchange, collective decision-making and shared responsibility in love and struggle, a relationship will fail to be meaningful and mutually beneficial (Karenga, 1980: 47-48).

Building and maintaining positive relationships requires guidance and strategies. Numerous social scientists have offered approaches to strengthening Black male-female relationships (Aldridge, 1984; Braithwaite, 1981; Cheek, 1977; Hare and Hare, 1989; Karenga, 1982; Myers, 1980; Rodgers-Rose and Rodgers, 1985; Young, 1989). Some of the strategies have been designed to deal more specifically at the interpersonal level, while others approach the institutional level. But, irrespective of the major focus, all social scientists concerned with Black male-female relationships have alluded to both interpersonal and institutional factors impacting these relationships.

Rodgers-Rose and Rodgers (1985) provide strategies for open communication, emphasizing the need to relate to each other through love, doing meaningful things together, knowing how to say "I'm sorry" as well as when to say no or set limits and keeping thoughts and behavior in the here and now. Tucker (1979) suggests that women can help strengthen relationships by communicating to men that they measure manhood not in terms of "coolness" but in terms of responsiveness, support, care, and honesty. Additionally, Black women can further help by encouraging Black men to struggle to cope with their emotions rather than conceal them. Black women need to share with Black men an assurance that a man is found more attractive when he shares his feeling with his partner. While Black men may complain about women who force them to deal with issues, Tucker concludes, ultimately they respect such a woman far more than they do a meek, compliant one who makes no demands.

It is important to add to Tucker's observations and suggestions the risk of rejection that Black men face when they share their feelings or express their emotions. Self-disclosure cuts both ways, involving risktaking from both parties. Self-disclosure can be particularly risky in relationships where unnecessary gameplaying exists. Burgest and Goosby (1985) advocate the exposure of games to achieve more meaningful relationships. Cheek (1977) addresses the need for assertiveness in the relationships of Black males and females. In his book, *Assertive Black-Puzzled White,* he provides an "assertive" training approach that translates the psychological theories of personality and counseling into an Afrocentric frame of reference.

> For African-Americans, then, one of the best definitions of assertiveness is an honest, open and direct verbal or non-verbal expression which does not have the intent of putting someone down...The intention of the assertive African-American person should be the basis of judgment, not the response of the target person (Cheek, 8).

The importance of positive interaction patterns is fundamental for "Blacks, who, like everyone else, benefit from guidance in choosing more productive and satisfying ways of relating to each other – and/or relating to those who are not Black" (Cheek, 8).

An additional strategy for building healthy relationships is found in Young's essay, "Psychodynamics of Coping and Surviving for the African American Female in a Changing World." Young (1989) contends that on an individual basis, the African American woman has an equal responsibility to select a partner who affirms her strengths, capabilities, and potential. The complementary nature of the support provided by each member of the relationship sustains a resilience and positive assertion of love, respect, and trust that is enabling rather than diminishing. This selectivity of a mate points to a very significant strategy: shared expectations upon entering relationships is pivotal to sustaining ongoing positive interaction among a man and woman. Rodgers-Rose (1980) has studied the qualities desired in males and females that should influence selectivity of a mate. Her study indicates that if we are to begin to understand the relationship between Black men and women, or women and men in general, we must move beyond the outer status (occupation, income, education, sexual compatibility) to inner qualities. The men and women in her sample were concerned about qualities such as understanding, honesty, warmth, dress, respectability, open communication, sharing, independence, knowing how to listen, dominance, selfishness, lying, fidelity, maturity, physical violence, affection, and cleanliness. If these areas of concern are contemplated when selecting and maintaining a mate, then an effective strategy would be to constantly evaluate these with potential and current mates.

A number of writers have focused upon strategies for healthy development of Black male and female children. They understand the process of socialization and maintain that it is during childhood that the shaping of present and future relationships between the two sexes is crucial. Such writers as Hale (1982), Hare and Hare (1985), Kunjufu (1984), Lewis (1988) and Wilson (1978) have been very forceful in positions taken on countering socialization practices which are negative to the survival and healthy development of Black children.

Kunjufu advocates in *Countering the Conspiracy to Destroy Black Boys* a program to provide skill development and recreation similar to the Boys Scouts with two major differences. He writes:

> The first is ideological. The political/historical persuasion of the Boy Scouts is the maintenance of the status quo, which in America is European-American male supremacy. The Simba's major thrust is to equip African-American boys ideologically with the tools to understand why Africans are oppressed and specifically African-American boys. If this objective is not met, the conspiracy will continue. In order to resist, you must first know what you're resisting. The second major difference is the distinction between self-directed learning and training. Boy Scouts, like most schools, train African-American children. There are fundamental differences between training and education....The Boy Scouts train boys to maintain America, the Simba program educates

71

boys to remove the injustices of racism, capitalism, sexism, and to fuel liberation and the maximization of human potential (1984, 33).

The Simba Program, resting on the above philosophy, includes strategies for parents and educators for the development of healthy Black males (Kunjufu, 1984: 34-35). Similarly, Kunjufu recommends additional approaches for Black child development that lead to healthy Black adults in *Developing Positive Self-Images and Discipline in Black Children.*

Hare and Hare (1985), like Kunjufu, have developed a strategy for the development of the Black male. In their book, *Bringing the Black Boy to Manhood: The Passage*, they outline a process through which Black boys should pass. This passage should result in the boy having an understanding of self and the immediate and extended families. And, as important as those two facets of existence are, the process of moving the Black boy to manhood entails much more and culminates in a formal ceremony – the Celebration.

While Hare and Hare and Kunjufu focus on Black male children, both of their works carry grave implications for Black female development. Yet, Mary Lewis (*Herstory: Black Female Rites of Passage*) and Nsenga Warfield-Coppock, Mafori Moore, Gwen Akua Gilyard, and Karen King (*Transformations: A Rites of Passage Manual for African American Girls*) provide greater vision toward enhancing the lives of African American females. As a whole, the strategies described by all of these authors focus upon males and females in childhood and adulthood. The emphasis in adulthood is corrective and in childhood it is preventive. If Black children are socialized in a healthy, proactive fashion understanding, respecting, loving and appreciating themselves and their gender opposites, the foundation will exist for development and sustenance of healthy relationships in adulthood. In childhood and adulthood, these strategies embrace the interpersonal and institutional forces shaping individuals and their relationships – as do other strategies that many social scientists, intellectuals, practitioners, and concerned individuals recommend.

Finally, other strategies for promoting and developing healthy Black male-female relationships suggest (1) social scientists pose and explore researchable questions examining the context in which African American male/female relationships are embedded, (2) demographers focus attention on the scarcity of African-American males as a national phenomenen having potentially grave consequences for the race and having deleterious effects on African-American women, (3)African-American men and women address unsatisfactory interpersonal relationships by participating in personal growth and human relations group sessions, (4) K-12 focus on equity issues of males and females in textbooks, curriculum, and extracurricular activities, (5) universities develop/include a course on male and female relationships as a part of their general education curriculum, (6) African-American national organizations place on their program agenda the issue of strategies for strengthening relationships between Black women and men, and finally, (7) religious, political, educational and social groups establish and promote consciousness-raising among males comparable to that obtained for women. If both Black men and women buy into these prescriptions, then, our survival and growth as a people most likely will be assured.

CONCLUSION:

A MACROANALYTICAL FRAMEWORK AND BEYOND

The foundation for a macroanalytical framework has been established in the preceding chapters. The interconnected variables of institutional capitalism, racism, sexism, and the Judeo-Christian ethic have been combined in a single term: institutionalized oppressive ideology. The various outcomes of this ideology have been illustrated to explain a significant degree of behavior within the macroanalytical framework.

In disaggregating the components of institutionalized oppressive ideology, the common theme of the superior status associated with one of two parties has been determined. In the case of capitalism, there is the owners-workers relationship. Racism maintains White over Black, while sexism allots the superior status to men over women. And, finally, the theme in the Judeo-Christian ethic as translated in this society places white males in a superior position to all other race-gender groups.

American society is defined by and developed from these four major structural and value systems – capitalism, racism, sexism, and the Judeo-Christian ethic. This macrosystem forms the basic framework for understanding the interpersonal dynamics of Black male-female relationships. It would not suffice, however, to simply cite these four ideological institutions with their various manifestations as the macrosystem upon which scholars and other concerned individuals need to focus their attention. Several tasks remain to be accomplished: (1) a series of research hypotheses need to be developed that will enable us to empirically cite the incidence of those roles and role behaviors which exemplify relationships influenced by the four ideological institutions; (2) hypotheses need to be generated and tested that demonstrate the interrelation of institutions and specific individual and dyadic behavior; (3) the research designs that are developed to test the hypotheses must enable the investigator to derive a descriptive demography that contains incidence and frequency data; and (4) we must discover how Black males and females within specific age groups distributed in varied socioeconomic strata evidence interpersonal behaviors influenced by the four concepts designated in the theoretical framework.

These seminal questions cannot be properly answered external to the framework of a macroanalytical theory. Thus, this task forms the corpus of the next generation of research

– one that encompasses *what has been said* about Black male-female relationships as well as *what can be said* about Black male-female relationships. Given this scholarly behavior, one suspects that we will find that Black male-female relationships operate on a continuum between rewarding and punishing behaviors and outcomes. The Black community, as well as other communities within American society, will not have to depend upon selected slices of Black reality. There will be, then, empirical grounds for a broad presentation of Black interpersonal heterosexual reality that serves as a guide for socialization and re-socialization, if the latter be needed, to increase the positive qualities of Black life in America. Joseph White, in *The Psychology of Blacks*, encapsulates the essence of the positive Black male-female relationship in the following description:

> The ideal male-female relationship within extended family networks and in the Black community at large would be one characterized by the [traditional] Afro-American values of interdependence, cooperation, and mutual respect, without a fixed classification of household, economic, and social responsibilities based on sex. Male-female relationships that are built on a bond of sharing, nurturance, tenderness, and appreciation have the strong psychological foundation necessary to cope with the social and economic stresses that usually confront Black couples living in a country dominated by Euro-Americans (1984, 73).

This book is grounded in the understanding that no society can be analyzed without a knowledge of the past and present status of its men and women. The institutional and interpersonal dimensions of the lives of men and women must be studied for a broad understanding of their relationships. The interplay of both forms the basis for the development of a macroanalytical theory for understanding Black male-female relationships. Society, with its institutional arrangements, influences significantly the interaction between Black men and women. The racism, sexism, capitalism, and Judeo-Christian ethic has impacted differentially upon Black males and females than it has for other race-gender groups within American society. The interplay of the structural or institutional aspects of Black life rooted in an oppressive ideology, as well as the psychological forces that individuals bring to intimate relationships, provides all the fundamental components necessary for "focusing" on the Black male-female dyad. Thus, any attempt to study male-female relationships among Black Americans that fails to place the interpersonal within the broad institutional context falls short of providing a macroanalytical model.

But, study and analysis, which is the first step, is not enough. Strategies for building and maintaining healthy relationships are crucial for the survival and development of people of African descent. The solution like the problem has both a personal and social dimension and requires transformation on both levels. And, while this work contends that social conditions create values of what relationships ought to be, both values and the behavior that they engender can and often do create the social conditions. Just as capitalism, racism, sexism and the Judeo-Christian ethic shape conflicts in Black male-female relationships, they are value systems which are created and maintained by humans – systems which can be transformed by humans. But neither personal nor social change is likely to occur without a belief in that possibility. Although the oppressive ideology that Blacks face in American society makes the task difficult, still it is possible. Black men and women must understand fully why their relationships are what they are and constructive steps must be taken to duplicate healthy relationships by teasing out the factors that contribute to their success. This must be done many thousand fold. It must be done *today* so that there will be a *tomorrow.*

SELECTED REFERENCES

Aldridge, D.P. *Sourcebook on Black Male-Female Relationships.* Dubuque, Iowa: Kendall/Hunt Publishing Company, 1989.

_____. "Toward an Understanding of Black Male/Female Relation ships," *The Western Journal of Black Studies,* Vol.8, No.4, 1984.

Asante, M.K. "Black Male and Female Relationship: An Afrocentric Context." In *Black Men,* L. E. Gary, editor, 75-82. Beverly Hills: Sage, 1981.

Anderson, S.E., and Mealy, R. "Who Originated the Crisis: A Historical Perspective." *Black Scholar* (May/June) 40-44.

Banks, J. A. and Grambs, J. *Black Self-Concept: Implications for Education and the Social Sciences.* New York: McGraw-Hill Book Company, 1972.

Barnes, A. S. *Black Women: Interpersonal Relationships in Profile.* Bristol, Indiana: Wyndham Hall Press, Inc., 1986.

Beale, Frances. "Double Jeopardy: To Be Black and Female." In *The Black Woman,* Toni Cade, editor. New York: New American Library, 1970.

Billingsley, A. "Black Families and White Social Science," *Journal of Social Issues,* Vol. 26, No. 3 (Summer) 127-142.

Braithewaite, R. L. "Interpersonal Relations Between Black Males and Black Females." In *Black Men,* L.E. Gary (ed.), Beverly Hills: Sage Publications, 1981.

Burgest, M.D.R. and M. Goosby. "Games in Black Male/Female Relationships." *Journal of Black Studies* (1985), Vol. 15, No. 3, 277-290.

Cazenave, N. A. "Black Male-Black Female Relationships: The Perceptions of 155 middle-class Black men." *Family Relations,* Vol. 32, 341-350, 1983.

Chapman, A. *Mansharing: Dilemma or Choice, A Radical New Way of Relating to the Men in Your Life.* New York: William Morrow and Co., 1986.

Chafetz, J. S. *Masculine/Feminine or Human?: An Overview of the Sex Roles.* Itasca, Illinois: F. E. Peacock Publishers, Inc. 1974.

Cheek, D.K. *Assertive Black ... Puzzled White.* San Luis Obispo: Impact Publishers, Inc., 1977.

Collier-Watson, B.C., W.D. Williams and L.N. Williams. "Differential Economic Status of Black Men and Women: Perception Versus Reality" in *Papers in the Social Sciences*, 1984, Vol. 4:47-60.

Cooley, C. H. *Social Organization.* New York: Scribners, 1909.

Duberman, L. *Gender and Sex in Society.* New York: Praeger, 1975.

Fanon, F. *Black Skin, White Masks.* New York: Grove Press, 1967.

Franklin, C. W. "White Racism As A Cause of Black Male Female Conflict: A Critique." *Western Journal of Black Studies* Vol.4, No. 1, 42-49.

_____. "Black Male-Black Female Conflict: Individually Caused and Culturally Nurtured," *Journal of Black Studies*, 1984, Vol. 15, No. 2 (December), 139-154, reprinted in *The Black Family: Essay and Studies.* Robert Staples, editor. Third Edition. Belmont, California: Wadsworth Publishing Company, Inc., 1986, 106-113.

Gary, L. E., editor. *Black Men.* Beverly Hills: Sage Publications, 1981.

_____. "Black Male-Female Relationships: An Empirical Assessment," *Proceedings of the Society for the Study of Social Problems,* 1985.

Gordon, V. V. *Black Women, Feminism, and Black Liberation: Which Way?* Chicago: Third World Press, 1985.

Grant, J. "Black Women and the Church." In G. T. Hull, P. B. Scott and B. Smith, editors. *All the Women Are White, All the Blacks Are Men, But Some of Us Are Brave.* Old Westbury, N.Y.: The Feminist Press, 1982, pp. 141-152.

Hale, J. *Black Children: Their Roots, Culture, and Learning Styles.* Provo Utah: Brigham Young University Press, 1982.

Hare, N. and Hare, J., editors. *Crisis in Black Sexual Politics.* San Francisco: Black Think Tank, 1989.

_____. *Bringing the Black Boy to Manhood: The Passage.* San Francisco: The Black Think Tank, 1985.

Harrison, A. "Dilemma of Growing Up Black and Female," *Journal of Social and Behavioral Sciences,* 1974.

Jackson, J. "But Where Are the Black Men?" *Black Scholar* (1971) Vol. 4,: 34-41.

_____. "Black Women in a Racist Society." In *Racism and Mental Health,* Willie, C., B. Kramer, and B. Brown (eds.). Pittsburgh: University of Pittsburgh Press, 1972.

Jourard, S. *The Transparent Self.* New York: jan Nostrand, 1971.

Karenga, M. *Introduction to Black Studies.* Inglewood, California: Kawaida Publications, 1982.

_____. *Beyond Connections: Liberation in Love and Struggle.* New Orleans: Ahidiana, 1978.

_____. *Kawaida Theory: An Introductory Outline.* Inglewood: Kawaida Publications, 1980.

King, M.C. "The Politics of Sexual Stereotypes." *The Black Scholar.* March-April 1973, 12-23.

Kunjufu, J. *Developing Positive Self-Images and Discipline in Black Children.* Chicago: African American Images, 1984.

_____. *Countering the Conspiracy to Destroy Black Boys.* Chicago: Afro-Am Publishing Co., 1984.

Ladner, J. *Tomorrow's Tomorrow: The Black Woman.* Garden City, New York: Doubleday and Co., 1971.

LaRue, L. Black Liberation and Women's Lib. *Transaction* (1970) Vol. 8, No. 1, 59-63.

Lewis, M.C. *Herstory: Black Female Rites of Passage*. Chicago: African American Images, 1988.

Liebow, E. *Tally's Corner: A Study of Negro Street Corner Men*. Boston: Little, Brown, 1967.

Lorde, A. "Feminism and Black Liberation." *The Black Scholar* (1979) Vol. 10, No. 8-9, 17-20.

Madhubuti, H. "Not Allowed To Be Lovers: Black Men and Women in the Struggle for Meaning, Family and Future," *Black Books Bulletin* Vol. 6 (Summer):48-57.

_____. *Black Men: Obsolete, Single, Dangerous?* Chicago: Third World Press, 1990.

_____. *Enemies: The Clash of Races*. Chicago: Third World Press, 1978.

_____. editor, *Confusion By Any Other Name: Essays Exploring the Negative Impact of The Blackman's Guide to Understanding the Black Woman*. Chicago: Third World Press, 1990.

Malveau, J. "Polar Entities Apart." *Essence Magazine* Vol. 4, 48-49.

Mannheim, K. *Ideology and Utopia*: An Introduction to the Sociology of Knowledge. New York: Harcourt, Brace & World, Inc. 1936.

Mead, G. H. *Mind, Self, and Society*. Chicago: University of Chicago Press, 1934.

Merton, R. K. *Social Theory and Social Structure*. 2nd Edition. Glencoe, Illinois: Free Press, 1957.

Myers, L. W. *Black Women Do They Cope Better?* New York: Prentice-Hall, 1980.

Pettigrew, T. "Racism and Mental Health of White Americans." In *Racism and Mental Health*. C. Willie, B. Kramer and B. Brown (eds.). Pittsburgh: University of Pittsburgh Press, 1973, 274-275.

Rodgers-Rose, L. (ed.) "Dialectics of Black Male-Female Relationships," *The Black Woman*. Beverly Hills: Sage Publications. 1980, 251-263.

_____, and J.T. Rodgers. *Strategies for Resolving Conflict in Black Male and Female Relationships.* Plainfield, New Jersey: Traces Institute Publications, 1985.

Salaam, K. "Revolutionary Struggle/ Revolutionary Love." *The Black Scholar* (1979) Vol. 10, No. 8-9, 20-24.

Scott, J. "Polygamy: A Futuristic Family Arrangement for African-Americans." *Black Books Bulletin* (1976), 13-19.

Sizemore, B. A. "Sexism and the Black Male," *The Black Scholar*, Vol. 4, No. 6-7, (March-April 1973), 2-11.

Staples, R. *The Black Woman in America.* Chicago: Nelson-Hall, 1973.

_____. "Masculinity and Race: The Dual Dilemma of Black Men." *Journal of Social Issues* (1978) Vol. 34, 168-183.

_____. "A Rejoiner: Black Feminism and the Cult of Masculinity, The Danger Within." *The Black Scholar* (1979) Vol. 10, 8-9.

_____. *The World of Black Singles: Changing Patterns of Male-Female Relations.* Westport, Conn: Greenwood Press, 1981.

_____. "Therapy to Quell the Rage: Love, Sex and Black Macho." *The Washington Post*, November 3, 1979.

_____. *Black Masculinity: The Black Male's Role in Society.* San Francisco: Black Scholar Press, 1982.

Tucker, R. "Why Do Black Men Hide Their Feelings?" *Essence*, September, 1978, p.4.

Wallace, M. *Black Macho and the Myth of the Superwoman.* New York: Dial Press, 1979.

Warfield-Coppock, N. , Moore, M. et al., *Transformations: A Rites of Passage Manual for African American Girls.* New York: Star Press, 1987.

_____. "A Black Feminist's Search for Sisterhood." In *All the Women Are White, All the Blacks Are Men, But Some of Us Are Brave*, G. T. Hull et al., (eds.), 5-8. Old Westbury, N. Y.:Feminist Press, 1982.

Wilkinson, D. and Taylor, R. *The Black Male In America.* Chicago: Nelson-Hall Publishers, 1977.

Wilson, A. *Developmental Psychology of the Black Child.* New York: Africana Research Publications, 1978.

White, J. *The Psychology of Blacks: An Afro-American Perspective.* Englewood Cliffs, N.J: Prentice-Hall, Inc., 1984.

Young, C. "Psychodynamics of Coping and Surviving of the African American Female in a Changing World," *Journal of Black Studies* (1989) Vol. 20, No. 2, 208-223.

ABOUT THE AUTHOR

Delores P. Aldridge is the Grace Towns Hamilton professor of Sociology and African American Studies at Emory University. She is also the founding director of African American and African Studies, which she has directed since its inception in 1971. She has served as executive director of the Greater LaFayette, Indiana Community Centers, Acting Director of Social Services at the Winter Haven, Florida Comprehensive Health Center, and Associate Director of the Tampa Urban League.

Recipient of a B.A. degree from Clark College, M.A. in Social Work from Atlanta University, Certificate in Child Psychology from the University of Ireland-Dublin, and the Ph.D. in Sociology from Purdue University, her research has focused on theoretical and empirical issues in Africana Studies, families and women's studies. Dr. Aldridge has authored several volumes on intergroup relations. Among her many articles and essays are those included in special guest edited issues of *Phylon: Review of Race and Culture* and *Journal of Black Studies*. She is the recipient of numerous awards, including Emory's Teaching Excellence Award in 1984, the W.E. B. DuBois Award from the Association of Social and Behavioral Scientists in 1986, an outstanding Alumni Award from Purdue University in 1988, and the Presidential Award from the National Council for Black Studies in 1989.

ALSO AVAILABLE FROM THIRD WORLD PRESS

Harvesting New Generations: The Positive Development Of Black Youth
by Useni Eugene Perkins
$12.95

Explosion Of Chicago Black Street Gangs
by Useni Eugene Perkins
$6.95

The Psychopathic Racial Personality And Other Essays
by Dr. Bobby E. Wright
$5.95

Black Women, Feminism And Black Liberation: Which Way?
by Dr. Vivian V. Gordon
$5.95

Black Rituals
by Sterling Plumpp
$8.95

The Redemption Of Africa And Black Religion
by St. Clair Drake
$6.95

How I Wrote Jubilee
by Margaret Walker
$1.50

Focusing: Black Male/Female Relationships
by Delores P. Aldridge
$7.95

Kemet and Other Ancient African Civilizations : Selected Readings
by Dr. Vivian V. Gordon
$3.95

Fiction

Mostly Womenfolk And A Man Or Two: A Collection
by
Mignon Holland Anderson
$5.95

ALSO AVAILABLE FROM THIRD WORLD PRESS

A Move Further South
by Ruth Garnett
$7.95

Manish
by Alfred Woods
$8.00

*New Plays for the Black
Theatre* (Anthology)
edited by Woodie King, Jr.
$14.95

Wings Will Not Be Broken
Darryl Holmes
$8.00

Jiva Telling Rites
Estella Conwill Majozo
$8.00

Sortilege (Black Mystery)
by Abdias do Nascimento
$2.95

Manish
by Alfred Woods
$8.00

Children's Books

*The Day They Stole
The Letter J*
by Jabari Mahiri
$3.95

*The Tiger Who Wore
White Gloves*
by Gwendolyn Brooks
$6.95

A Sound Investment
by Sonia Sanchez
$2.95

*Afrocentric Self Inventory
and Discovery Workbook*
by Useni Perkins
$5.95

I Look At Me
by Mari Evans
$2.50

The Story of Kwanzaa
by Safisha Madhubuti
$5.95